Preface

French for Kids 3 is a series of 3 course books. This is the third part for the earliest stage of learning French as a foreign language where students are able to understand some rules of their maternal language. This book is useful in the primary schools of India and abroad. This is intended to help the beginners and the parents to prepare their kids to start learning French as foreign language. This book provides a simple and interesting method of teaching to teachers and different ways of learning French to the students with an innovative approach.

This book should be of value as this book is integrated with pictorial representations for better visual learning experience for the kids. In this book for the better understanding of our students, every topic has different exercises for practice which can gives confidence to the students.

At the end, I would like to say that the book is designed to equip both the teachers and the students with ideal guidance and exercises for practice.

Table of Contents

Preface....1

Lesson 1 (Leçon 1): We are in France. (Nous sommes en France.)....3

Lesson 2 (Leçon 2): Speak the correct pronunciation (Parlez la pronunciation correcte)....11

Lesson 3 (Leçon 3): It's four O'clock...minutes. (Il est quatre heures.....minutes?.)....18

Lesson 4 (Leçon 4): 'You' or 'You'. ('Tu' ou 'Vous'.)....21

Lesson 5 (Leçon 5) : Introduce yourself. (Présentez–vous.)....24

Lesson 6 (Leçon 6): I am a king. (Je suis un roi.)....27

Lesson 7 (Leçon 7): I speak, listen, sing, etc. (Je parle, écoute, chante..etc.)....31

Lesson 8 (Leçon 8): Let's go to Super market (Allons au super marché)....33

Lesson 9 (Leçon 9): What are you doing? (Qu'est-ce que tu fais ?)....35

Lesson 10 (Leçon 10): Wow ! It's raining. (Oh là là! il pleut.)....37

Answers (Les réponses)....41

Lesson 1 (Leçon 1): We are in France. (Nous sommes en France.)

Hello friends, I am Shizuka, I am from Japan. Today my father and I are in France. According to our plan, we arrived in Paris this morning. Since then, we have visited the city to see different museums and monuments.

A museum is a building or an institution that cares for and displays a collection of artefacts and other objects of artistic, cultural, historical, or scientific importance where we can conserve thecountry's heritage.
Some famous museums of Paris are:

Museum of Orsay

Musée d'Orsay

This museum is situated on the left bank of the Seine river. It was officially opened in 1986; earlier it was a railway station also known as Gare d'Orsay.

Grevin museum

Musée de Grévin

This is a wax museum that was founded on June 5, 1882. It consists of a collection of wax sculptures representing famous people and personalities from history.

Louvre museum

Musée du Louvre

This museum is situated on the right bank of the Seine river. It was founded in 1793, earlier it was a castle also known as the Medieval Louvre. It displays one of the most famous paintings it the world called "Mona Lisa" made by Leonardo da Vinci. Now, Let's talk about monuments.

Monument is an old building or statue that is built to remind people of a famous person or event of historical importance.

Some famous monuments of Paris are:

Eiffel tower

Tour Eiffel

This is Eiffel tower, the tallest structure in Paris made up of wrought iron. The height of this tower is 330 meters with 81 storeys.

Triumphal arc

Arc de triumphe

The Triumphal arch honors those who fought and died for France during the French Revolution 1789.

Palace garnier

Opéra garnier

This is the most famous opera house in the world. There is no price to visit the Paris Opera House, that is free for children under 12 years of age.

Shizuka: Today, we visited many different museums and monuments in Paris. Now, we are planning further to visit other cities in France

By using various means of transport.

Let's talk about different means of transport in France.
There are four means of transports depending on the route you take.
1. Road transport
2. Sea transport
3. Rail transport
4. Air transport

1. Road transport

Bus - Car

There are numerous bus lines and many buses go through the centre of the city, along the banks of the Seine, and through historic districts etc. Buses can be used to travel within a city or to go from one city to another.

Bicycle - Vélo

Vélib' Métropole is a large-scale public bicycle sharing system in Paris, France. It is one of the best means of transport for tourists to travel within Paris.

Car -Voiture

Taxis G7 is the No. 1 taxi service in Europe and the taxi leader in Paris and it has more than 9500 taxis in its network.

2. Sea transport

There are four water bodies in France:

1) The Northern Sea
2) English Channel
3) Atlantic Ocean
4) Mediterranean Sea.

There are some places in France where one can enjoy a boat ride to explore a region within the city. You can also find some yachts in the coastal areas and ships which are used to travel through sea routes from one country to another.

To visit different cities in France we use:

1) Ships

Ship - Bateau

2) Yacht

Yacht- Yacht

3) Boats

Boat –Bateau

3. Rail transport

The train is the cheapest, easiest and fastest way to get around Paris. Children until 14 years of age can travel for free. One can use trains to travel through different cities within France.

France has four train companies that provide only domestic routes.

These companies are:

1) SNCF

2) TGV

3) OUIGO

4) RER

The **SNCF** is known to be the main operator of trains in France.

Le Petit Train Jaune is the most famous vintage train ride.

There are 16 metro lines and around 300 metro stations. The entrance is indicated by a large yellow letter 'M'.

4. Air transport

France is one of the largest aviation markets in Europe with some of the most famous airlines such as Air France and Airbus. France has 136 airports from which one can take flights in inside and outside of France.

Some famous airports of France are ;

1) Paris Charles de Gaulle Airport

2) Lyon-Saint Exupéry Airport

3) Toulouse-Blagnac Airport

À Vous

Exercise 1: Write down the names of the museums of Paris in French. (Any two)

Exercise 2: Write down the names of the monuments of Paris in French. (Any two)

Exercise 3: Write down the modes of transport in French.

Exercise 4: Write down the names of road transport in French. (Any two)

Exercise 5: Write down the names of train companies in France. (Any two)

Exercise 6: Fill in the blanks.

1. __________________ is a building or institution that displays a collection of artefacts and other objects of artistic, cultural, historical, or scientific importance.
2. __________________ is an old building or statue that is built to remind people of a famous person or event of historical importance.
3. ______________________________________ is the most famous vintage train ride.
4. No need to pay any fare for the kids under 14 in ____________________________.
5. ____ is the tallest structure of France.
6. With the grace of ___________________ we can lend bicycle to go nearby places.
7. No need to pay any fare for the kids under 12 in ____________________________.
8. There are ____________________ metro lines and ______________metro stations.

Lesson 2 (Leçon 2): Speak the correct pronunciation (Parlez la pronunciation correcte)

Today Shizuka is visiting markets in France. She wants to buy some bread. It is written "Pain" with the image of bread. It was surprising for her. As in English pain is a problem faced by someone in the body or after getting wounded. She eventually realized that the way we pronounce "Pain" in French is completely different from English. Now she sees so many words of the sound **"ain"** around her.

Bath-

Bain

Bread-

Pain

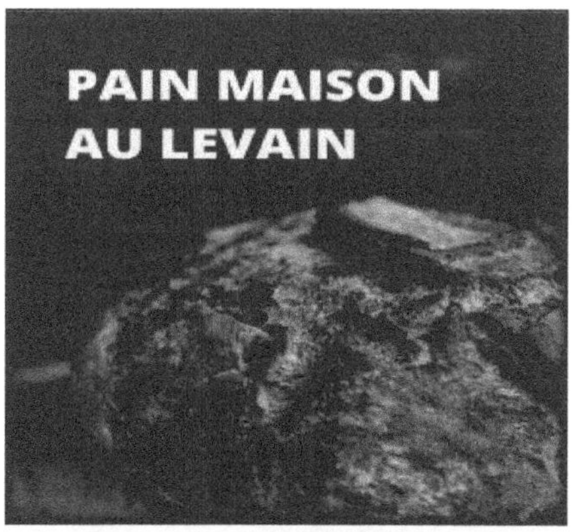

Hand-

Main

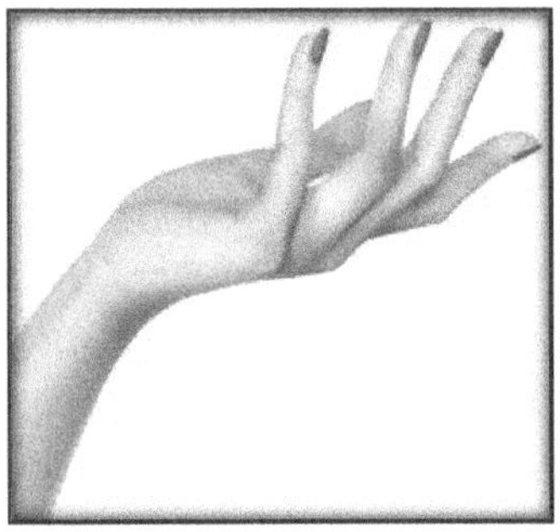

Dwarf-

Nain

She visits a cafeteria. There, she sees the menu and wants to order fish. She notices that the word "Poisson" for fish is written on the menu. She again gets confused about how to pronounce the word. She was only familiar with the word "Poisson" in English. Eventually she understood that the pronunciation of "Poisson" in French is completely different from "Poisson" in English. Some other French words with **"oi"** sound are:

Fish-

Poisson

Peas-

Pois

Me-

Moi*

Month-

Mois*

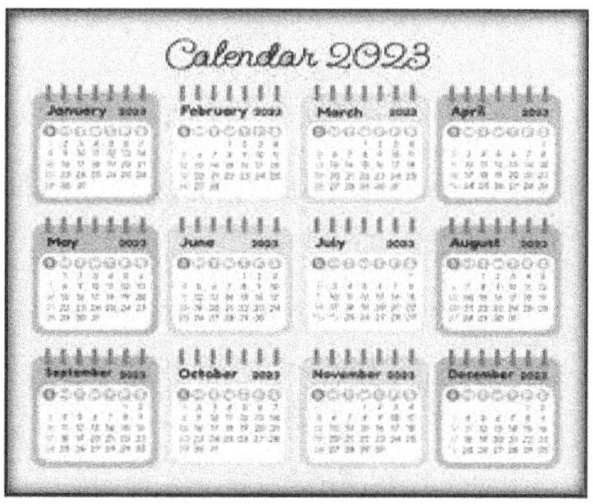

Less-

Moins*

*Note : The three words “moi”, “mois”, and “moins” have the same pronunciation but different meanings.

Wood-

Bois

To drink-

Boire

Some people in the cafeteria could see her wondering and facing difficulty. One man comes to her and greet her by saying “Bonjour petite fille!”

After hearing that “fille” word she thinks about “fee” like school fee. Again shocked, “What the man is saying?” Words of sound **“ill”**

Girl-

Fille

City-

Ville

Size-

Taille

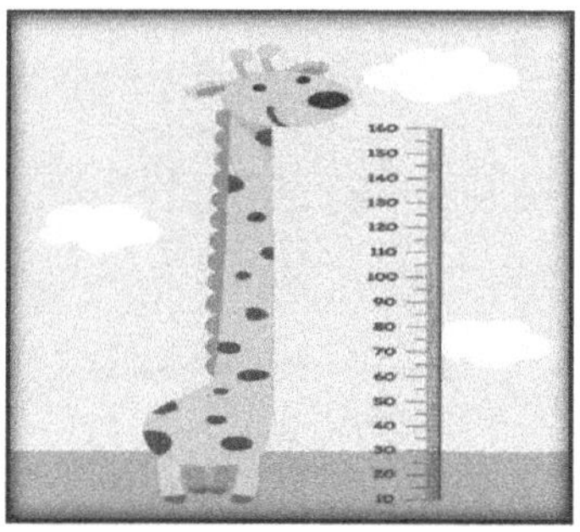

Leaf-

Feuille

Family-

Famille

To wake up

Réveiller

Note: For the better understanding the teacher can share some more words during the session.

À Vous

Exercise 1: Write some 'Ain' sound words.
Exercise 2: Write some 'Oi' sound words.
Exercise 3: Write some 'ill' sound words.
Exercise 4: Match with correct image.

Taille	
Pain	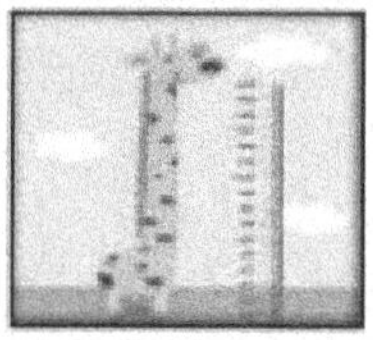
Poisson	
Ville	
Feuille	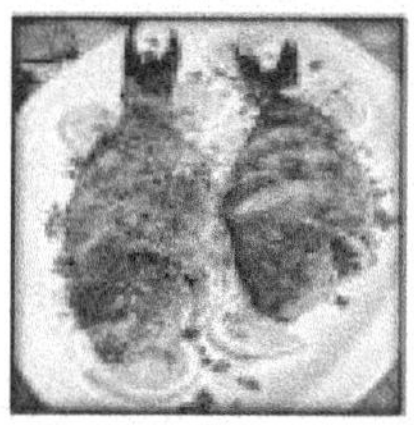

Exercise 5 : Choose the correct answer.

A) January is......................................

(i) Moins (ii) Mois (iii) Moi

B) Leaf is......................................

(i) Feuille (ii) Fille (iii) Mille

C) Dwarf is......................................

(i) Bois (ii) Nain (iii) Mille

D) Less is......................................

(i) Moins (ii) Nain (iii) Mille

E) Wood is......................................

(i) Pois (ii) Ville (iii) Bois

F) Bath is......................................

(i) Poisson (ii) Bain (iii) Moins

Lesson 3 (Leçon 3): It's four O'clock...minutes. (Il est quatre heures.....minutes?.)

Shizuka and her father are travelling by metro in France. As they move inside the metro station, Shizuka sees a clock showing the time "16:30". She gets confused because in Japan people only have 12 hours in a clock.

Her father explained to her that in France, they have 24 hours format of telling time and "16:30" means "4:30".

Now, she knows the correct format but still doesn't know how to say it in French. She asks her father for help.

Shizuka	:	Papa, I know numbers up to 20 in French but I don't know how to tell time in French.
Papa	:	Don't worry my dear. I will tell you.
Papa	:	For that you have to learn more numbers to indicate time.
Shizuka	:	Yes papa, I will learn more numbers after 20.

The Numbers 21-60 (Les nombres 21-60)

21	vingt-et-un	31	trente-et-un	41	quarante-et-un	51	cinquante-et-un
22	vingt-deux	32	trente-deux	42	quarante-deux	52	cinquante-deux
23	vingt-trois	33	trente-trois	43	quarante-trois	53	cinquante-trois
24	vingt-quatre	34	trente-quatre	44	quarante-quatre	54	cinquante-quatre
25	vingt-cinq	35	trente-cinq	45	quarante-cinq	55	cinquante-cinq
26	vingt-six	36	trente-six	46	quarante-six	56	cinquante-six
27	vingt-sept	37	trente-sept	47	quarante-sept	57	cinquante-sept
28	vingt-huit	38	trente-huit	48	quarante-huit	58	cinquante -huit
29	vingt-neuf	39	trente-neuf	49	quarante-neuf	59	cinquante-neuf
30	trente	40	quarante	50	cinquante	60	soixante

Let's see how to tell time in French in minutes.
As you learnt It is one o'clock – Il est une heure. It is two o'clock – Il est deux heures. But If "It is 5 minutes past one" OR "1:05" Then « Il est une heure cinq. » If "It is 10 minutes past one" OR "1:10" Then « Il est une heure dix. » If "It is 20 minutes past one" OR "1:20" Then « Il est une heure vingt. » If "It is 35 minutes past one" OR "1:35" Then « Il est une heure trente-cinq. »
That is the easiest way to tell time in minutes. Something more to learn :

If "It is 15 minutes past one" OR "1:15"
Then « Il est une heure quinze. » OR « Il est une heure et *quart*[*]. »

If "It is 30 minutes past one" OR "1:30"

Then « Il est une heure trente. » OR « Il est une heure et *demie*[**]. »

If "It is 45 minutes past one" OR "1:45"
Then « Il est une heure quarante-cinq. » OR« Il est deux heures *moins le quart.*[***] »

*	Quatre past
**	Half past....
***	Quatre to...

For midnight 12:00	Il est miniuit.
For noon 12:00	Il est midi.

À Vous

Exercise 1: What is the time in clock?

	________________________________
	________________________________
	________________________________
	________________________________
	________________________________
	________________________________

Exercise 2: Write the number names in French.

1. 46 ________________________________
2. 32 ________________________________
3. 28 ________________________________
4. 53 ________________________________
5. 60 ________________________________

Lesson 4 (Leçon 4): 'You' or 'You'. ('Tu' ou 'Vous'.)

Today, Shizuka was playing with her friend Aline in the park. Suddenly, she noticed their teacher passing by with her 8 years old son Joseph. Shizuka and Aline decided to go and greet them.

Aline	:	Bonjour madame ! Vous allez bien ?
Teacher	:	Bonjour les filles ! Oui, je vais bien, et vous ?
Aline	:	Nous allons bien madame.
Joseph	:	Salut Aline ! Oui, je vais bien.
Teacher	:	Au revoir !
Aline and Shizuka	:	Au revoir madame !

After the conversation, Shizuka seemed a bit lost in her thoughts. Aline asked Shizuka how she could help her. Shizuka explained her that she has problem using 'Tu' and 'Vous' in French. She further asked her why she used 'Vous' while greeting teacher but used 'Tu' while greeting Joseph and why their teacher addressed them 'Vous' instead of 'Tu'.

Aline explains that in French both "Tu' and 'Vous' mean 'You', but they use 'Tu' to address people younger than you or your friends, while 'Vous' is used to address strangers or elders and also when we need to address more than one person.

Tu (Singular) - Younger people, friends.
Vous (Singular/Plural) – Elders, strangers, more than one person.

Pronouns

I, We, You, He, She, It, They

These pronouns replace a noun or nouns in the naming part of a sentence. Now you are going to learn the same in French.

	I		WE
	YOU		YOU
	HE		THEY
	SHE		THEY

In the table, “You” is mentioned two times.

Tu you Informal.
Vous you Formal.

So, don’t use “Tu” with elders and strangers.
Always use “Vous” with elders and strangers.
As per table plurals will be as follows:

Singular (Singulier)	Plural (Pluriel)
I(Je)	We(Nous)
You(Tu)	You(Vous)
He(Il)	They(Ils)
She(Elle)	They(Elles)

À Vous

Exercise 1: Match the coloumns.

	Nous
	Ils
	Je
	Tu
	Il

Lesson 5 (Leçon 5) : Introduce yourself. (Présentez–vous.)

Today it's Sunday. Shizuka is going to the park to have fun on rides and swings. She is playing alone. After few minutes a French girl came to her and started conversation.

	Salut ! Salut ! Je m'appelle Salina. J'habite à Paris. Et toi, comment tu t'appelles ?	
I am really sorry but I am not able to understand whatever you are trying to say. I can't understand French. I am from Japan.		Attends !

A few minutes later, Slina takes Shizuka to her class where she can get some help.

Now teacher is telling the students how to introduce themselves in front of anyone.

She is using both languages.

- My name is Shizuka.
  Je m'appelle Shizuka.
- I am 10 yrs old.
  J'ai dix ans.
- I live in Japan.
  J'habite au Japon.
- I am Japanese.
  Je suis japonaise.
- I am intelligent.
  Je suis Intelligente.

Shizuka is doing speaking practice in the class.
Now she can make some new friends in France.

After meeting with her new friends, she went back to her father and told each and everything that had happened in the park and class. She is presenting herself in front of her father.

There are some points to describe you. The correct order of sentences has to be followed.

- Start by name.
- Tell the age.
- Tell the place where you live.
- Tell the nationality.
- Use describing words as per your gender.

Look at the table how describing words change with number and gender.

Singular	Plural	Singular	Plural
 intelligent	 Intelligents	 intelligente	 intelligentes
 Grand	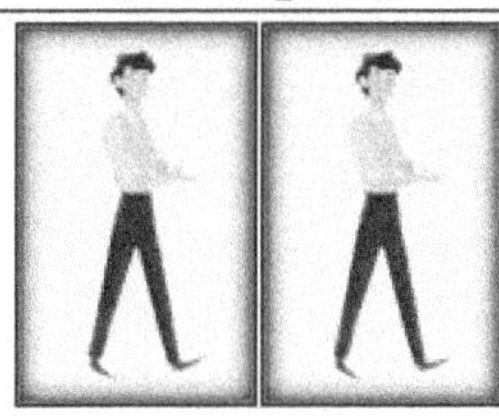 Grands	 Grande	 Grandes
 Gros	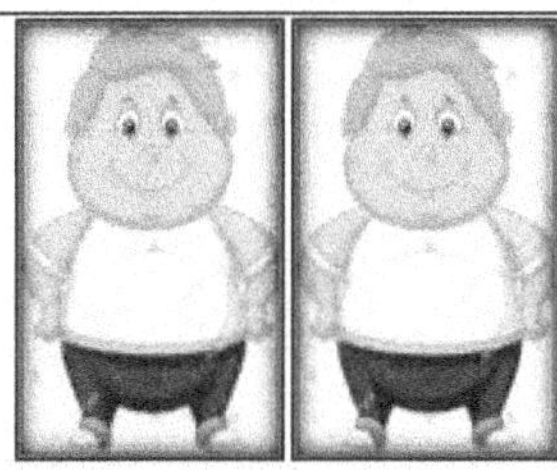 Gros	 Grosse	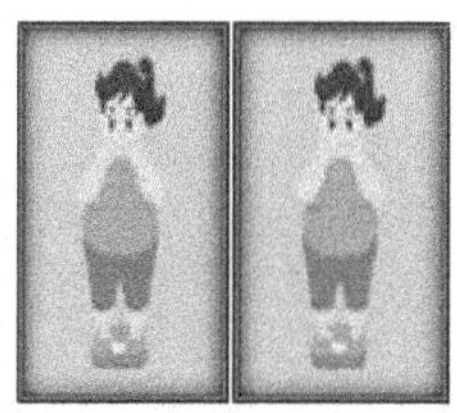 Grosse

 Petit	 Petits	 Petite	 Petites
 Beau	 Beaux	 Belle	 Belles

À Vous

Exercise 1: Describe yourself in French by using appropriate words according to your gender.

Exercise 2: Match with the correct describing words:

Belle	
Gros	
Grands	
Petites	
Intelligent	

Lesson 6 (Leçon 6): I am a king. (Je suis un roi.)

Today Shizuka is visiting some palaces of Paris and nearby champagnes. She visited old castles of Paris which were once ruled by French kings. She saw different types of old weapons in the exhibition. Some famous palaces are as follows:

Palace Of Versailles

The Palace of Versailles is a former royal residence built by King Louis XIV located in Versailles, about 19 kilometers west of Paris, France.

Luxembourg Palace

Luxembourg Palace is the most renowned tourist attraction that serves as the place of the Senate of the Fifth Republic.

Tuileries Palace

The Tuileries Palace was a royal and imperial palace in Paris which located on the right bank of the River Seine, directly in front of the Louvre.

Vincennes

Vincennes is a commune famous for its castle: The Château de Vincennes.

After visiting the places, she plays a game with her French friends in which she becomes the queen of France.

Her French friends help her in constructing the sentences in French. They are explaining, if she wants to describe herself, then she should use new words.

Like Être i.e "To be".

I am a king.	Je suis un roi.
I am a queen.	Je suis une reine.

I am a girl. Je suis une fille.

Now look at the table given below.

être (to be)

 I am	 We are

 He is	 They are
 She is	 They are

By acting like a queen, Shizuka is telling about the things she is has as a queen, like weapons, arms, a crown, etc.
Again her French friends explain her how to tell whatever you have as a student, as a girl, or as a king or queen.

They are telling her to use the verb "Avoir" ie. "To have" like
I have a weapon. J'ai une arme.
I have a crown. J'ai une couronne.
I have a cycle. J'ai un vélo.
I have a pen. J'ai un stylo.

They also explained her that she can use the verb "Avoir"to tell her age. Like:
I am 10 yr old. J'ai dix ans.
I am 25 yr old. J'ai vingt-cinq ans.

Now look at the table given below.

 I have	 We have
 You have	 You have
 He has	 They have
 She has	 They have

À Vous

Exercise 1: Fill the blanks with the help of "ÊTRE"

1. Elle .... française?
2. Je .... espagnol
3. Elle .... la mère de Marc
4. Alice .... anglaise
5. Nous .... des amis
6. Louis .... professeur.
7. Vous .... un bon élève
8. Anne et Alice .... très sympas

Exercise 2: Fill the blanks with the help of "AVOIR "

1. Elle .... 18 ans
2. J' .... 12 ans et il .... 8 ans
3. Alice .... deux chiens.
4. Nous .... une grande maison.
5. Louis et Paul .... un nouveau professeur.
6. Vous .... une guitare?

Lesson 7 (Leçon 7): I speak, listen, sing, etc. (Je parle, écoute, chante..etc.)

Shizuka is learning more new things from her French friends. Now, she wants to get schooling here in France. For that, her father takes her to a nearby school. There, she meets the teacher and shows interest in taking a class.

Teacher asks about her hobbies. Shizuka replies by saying singing, dancing, drawing etc. After seeing her excitement in school, the teacher allows her to sit in the class.
Now, the teacher asks John to show his drawing. And ask the French verb to draw. John replies 'Déssiner' The teacher's other question is the French word for dancing. Caroline replies 'Danser' One more question from the teacher is the French word for singing. Here Shizuka replies 'Chanter'.

Teacher	:	You all can observe here that these words are ending with "er".
Students	:	Yes ma'am!
Teacher	:	We have three groups of verbs in French: "er" ending, "ir" ending, "re" ending verbs.
Caroline	:	Ma'am, can you tell us some other examples of the verbs ending with "er"
Teachers	:	Yes, of course.

Now look at the table:

Écouter	To listen	
Chanter	To sing	

Jouer	To play	
Cuisnier	To cook	
Dessiner	To draw	

Just like above there are some more verbs like "Regarder", "Parler", "Trouver", etc. These verbs work with subject pronouns. That you will learn in the next level.

À Vous

Exercise 1: Find the given verbs from the grill.

W	E	Y	R	U	I	R	H	G	L	K	H
R	E	G	A	R	D	E	R	Q	W	F	L
S	F	H	É	D	E	M	A	N	D	E	R
M	N	V	C	O	M	P	T	E	R	L	V
S	F	H	O	J	A	L	U	R	O	P	Q
A	X	M	U	X	N	A	I	M	E	R	C
F	H	K	T	I	G	C	D	F	G	H	J
W	E	R	E	Y	U	E	I	O	P	K	L
D	F	G	R	H	R	R	J	K	L	S	A

Lesson 8 (Leçon 8): Let's go to Super market (Allons au super marché)

After getting admission to the school, Shizuka needs to purchase some items like a bag, bottle, tiffin, stationary items, etc.

Her father asks her to go to the supermarket where she can find all the things in the same place. On her way she meets her friend. She asks Shizuka, "Tu vas où ?" but Shizuka doesn't understand her question. Her friend explains to her that it means, "Where are you going?"

She also suggests Shizuka to visit "Carrefour" he biggest convenience store in her area. There, she can find everything she needs
Her friend also tells her that "Va" means "Going" which is the verb "Aller" which means "To go" in English.

After meeting her friend, she visited Carrefour. Carrefour City stores are convenience stores in city centre.They are open six days a week. After returning from the market she tells her father the new verb she learnt today and also makes sentences for practice.

I go to school. — Je vais à l'école.
You are going to market. — Tu vas au marché.
Where are you going? — Tu vas où ?

Note : We always use « à » after the verb 'Aller'

Now look at the table given below.

ALLER

Je vais I go / I am going	Nous allons We go / We are going
Tu vas You go / you are going	Vous allez You go / You are going
Il va He go / He is going	Ils vont They go / They are going
Elle va	Elles vont

À Vous

Exercise 1: Fill the blanks with the help of "ALLER "

1. Je _________ au cinéma.
2. Vous _________ à l'école sur l'internet.
3. Elles _________ à Bayshore pour magasiner.
4. Nous _________ à Québec pour nos vacances.
5. Tu _________ à Saint Hubert ce soir.
6. Il _________ au match des Sénateurs.
7. Vous _________ au parc.
8. Je _________ à Toronto.
9. Elles _________ à l'école chaque semaine.
10. Tu _________ manger la pizza!

Exercise 2: Write the names of some shopping stores of Paris.

Lesson 9 (Leçon 9): What are you doing? (Qu'est-ce que tu fais ?)

Today, Aline and some other friends have invited Shizuka to visit the sports complex of the city. There, Shizuka sees people doing different sports activities like swimming, tennis, judo, basketball, etc. They are discussing what activities they all like to do:

Aline- Je fais de la natation.

Julie-Je fais du ski.

Amanda-Je fais du vélo.

Aline-Et toi, Shizuka. Qu'est ce-que tu fais ?

Shizuka didn't understand the question and asked her friends what 'Fais' means. They explain to her that it's a French verb 'Faire' which means 'To do' or 'To make'.

We use the verb 'Faire' to tell our hobbies like which sports we play. It is also used to indicate the weather.

To tell the weather
Il fait beau. (The weather is pleasant.)
Il fait chaud. (It is hot.)
Il fait froid. (It is cold.)

To tell your hobbies
Je fais de la natation. (I do swimming.)
Je fait du vélo. (I do cycling.)
Je fais du gâteau. (I make cake.)

Now look at the following table:

 I am making a cake.	 We are doing homework.
 You are doing shopping.	 You are doing sports.

 It's pleasant weather.	 They are doing the dishes.

À Vous

Exercise 1: Fill the blanks with the help of "Faire".

	Je __________________du football.
	Elle__________________ du gâteau.
	Il ____________________du vélo.
	Nous ________________ les devoirs.
	Il ____________________beau.

Exercise 2: Write some different activities in French using the "Faire" word.

Lesson 10 (Leçon 10): Wow ! It's raining. (Oh là là! il pleut.)

Today, Shizuka is going to the park near her apartment. Her father ask her to carry something to protect herself from the rain. Shizuka refused to carry anything, as in the month of April, there isn't any rainfall in Japan.

She is going to the park. It is a sunny day, And the Children are playing. All of a sudden, it became dark. After a few minutes, it started raining and the children started to leave for their homes. Shizuka didn't have anything to protect herself from the rain.

She ran quickly towards her apartment and learnn to always follow her father's advice. The next day, she went to the supermarket and saw many valuable things that are useful during the rainy season, whether going to school, the park or the market.

Essentials items during rainy season (Les Articles essentiels pendant la mousson.)

Raincoat	Imperméable	
Umbrella	Parapluie	
Gumboots	Bottes en caoutchouc	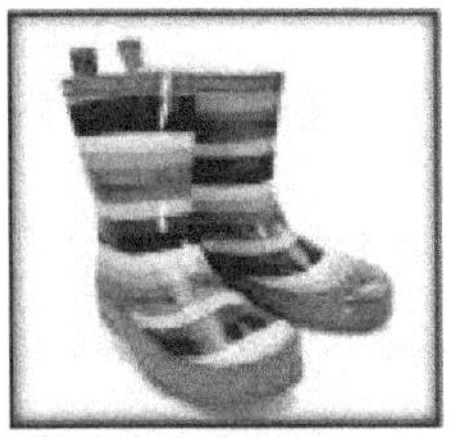
Backpack rain cover	Couverture arrière de pluie	

From now on everytime when she goes out, she follows the weather forecasting. In French it is known as 'La météo'.

Seasons (Les saisons)

After seeing forecasting of so many of days, Shizuka observed that there are four seasons in France.
1 - Spring (Le printemps)
2 - Summer (L'été)
3 - Autumn (L'automne)
4 - Winter (L'hiver)

1. Spring (Le printemps)

Spring season starts by the end of February or the beginning of March. During spring season, everyone feels pleasant, birds chirp and sing, we can see a lot of flowers blooming in the garden. The weather is neither too hot nor too cold during this season.

2. Summer (L'été)

Summer season starts by the end of May or the beginning of June. Everyone feels very hot and warm. Kids enjoy the summer vacations from school. Usually they spend their time near champagne or on the beaches. They also like to drink juices, cold drinks and eat ice-creams.

3. Autumn (L'automne)

Autumn in France is one of the loveliest times of the year. It starts at the end of September or the beginning of October. During this season, we feel cool winds and heavy rains. Trees shed their leaves. The colour of the sky changes to grey and black frequently.

4. Winter (Hiver)

This season starts at the end of November or the beginning of December. The temperature falls below zero degrees Celcius and the roofs of the houses covered with snow. Kids build snowman young people go skiing, elders sit near the fireplace, everyone likes to have hot soups.

À Vous

Exercise 1: What do we drink in winter?

(i) Hot soups (ii) Juices

Exercise 2: What do we wear in rain?

(i) Tee-shirt (ii) Impérmeable

Exercise 3: In France, when do we have loveliest time?

(i) Automne (ii) Hiver

Answers (Les réponses)

Leçon 1

Exercise 1: Musée d'Orsay ; Musée de Grévin (Answer may vary.)

Exercise 2: Tour Eiffel ; Arc de triomphe (Answer may vary.)

Exercise 3: Road transport ; Sea transport ; Rail transport ; Air transport

Exercise 4: Car ; Vélo (Answer may vary.)

Exercise 5: SNCF ; OUIGO (Answer may vary.)

Exercise 6: 1. A museum ; 2. A Monument ; 3. Le Petit Train Jaune ; 4. Train ; 5. Eiffel tower ; 6. Vélib ; 7. Palace garnier ; 8. 16 metro lines, 300 metro stations

Leçon 2

Exercise 1: Bain ; Main ; Pain ; Nain (Answer may vary.)

Exercise 2: Mois ; Bois ; Pois ; Poisson (Answer may vary.)

Exercise 3: Fille ; Mille ; Feuille ; Ville (Answer may vary.)

Exercise 4:

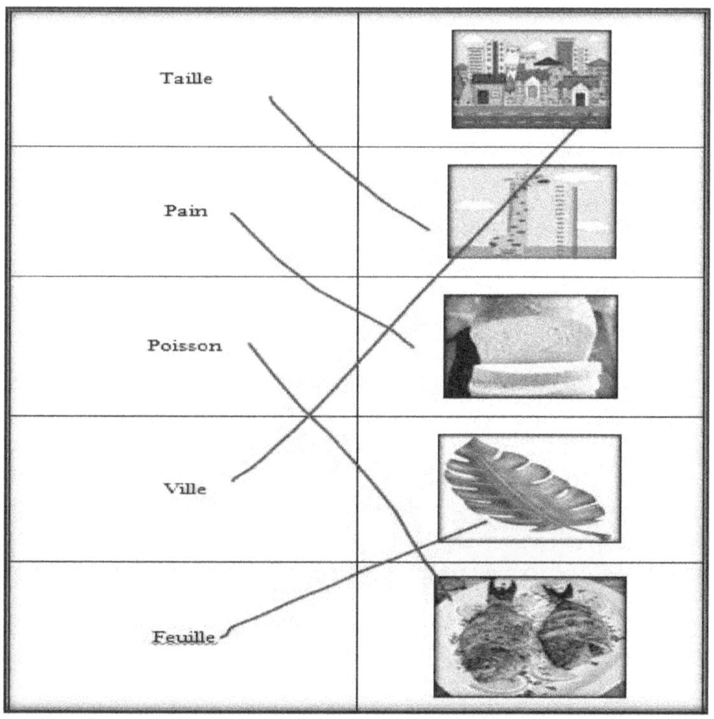

Exercise 5:

A (ii) Mois
B (i) Feuille
C (ii) Nain
D (i) Moins
E (iii) Bois
F (ii) Bain

Leçon 3

Exercise 1:

	Il est trois heures.
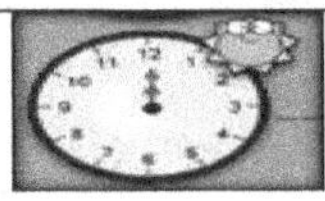	Il est midi.
	Il est minuit.
	Il est deux heures moins le quart.
	Il est onze heures et quart.
	Il est sept heures et demie.

Exercise 2: 1. quarante-six 2. trente-deux 3. vingt-huit 4. cinquante-trois   5. soixante

Leçon 4

Exercise 1:

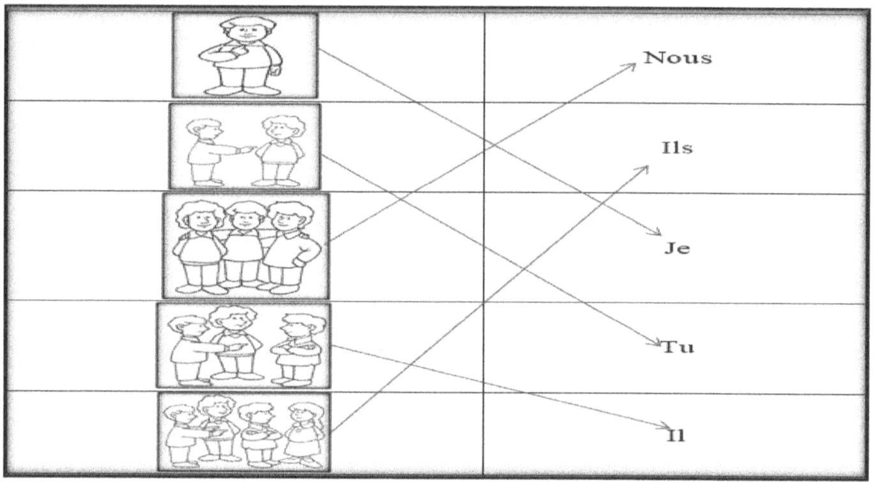

Leçon 5

Exercise 1: Answer may vary.

Exercise 2:

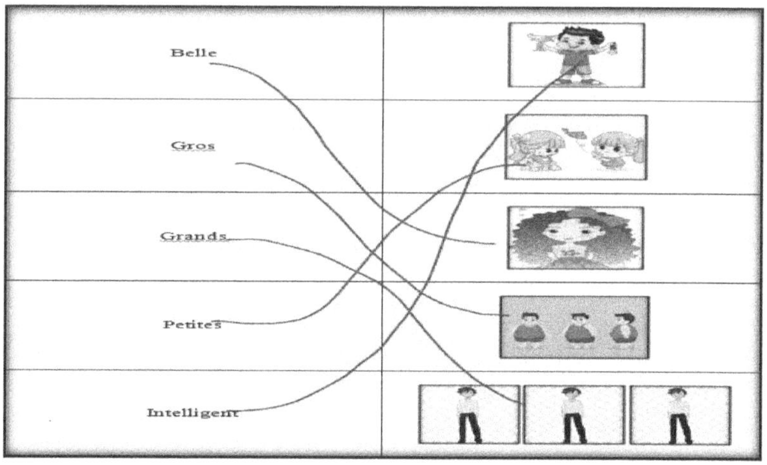

Leçon 6

Exercise 1:

1. est
2. suis
3. est
4. est
5. sommes
6. est
7. etes

8. sont

Exercise 2:

1. a
2. ai, a
3. a
4. avons
5. ont
6. avez

Leçon 7

Exercise 1:

						R					
R	E	G	A	R	D	E	R				
			É	D	E	M	A	N	D	E	R
			C	O	M	P	T	E	R		
			O		A	L					
			U		N	A	I	M	E	R	
			T		G	C					
			E		E	E					
			R		R	R					

Leçon 8

Exercise 1:

1. vais
2. allez
3. vont
4. allons
5. vas
6. va
7. allez
8. vais
9. vont
10. vas

Exercise 2: Bon marché ; Galeries lafayette (Answer may vary.)

Leçon 9

Exercise 1:

			Je _______fais_______ football.
			Elle_______fait_______ gateau.
			Il _______fait_______ vélo.
			Nous _______faisons_______ devoirs.
			Il _______fait_______ beau.

Exercise 2: Answer may vary.

Leçon 10

Exercise 1: (i) Hot soups

Exercise 2: (ii) Impermeable

Exercise 3: (iii) Automne

9 789369 917327

Printed at Repro India Ltd.